earth songs:
WINTER

POEMS BY PAULA MARTIN

EARTH SONGS PRESS
www.earthsongspress.com

Earth Songs Press

Library of Congress Cataloging-in-
Publication-Data has been applied for.

Illustrations by Sophia Morell

Printed in the United States of America
Print ISBN 978-0-9846199-3-1

Fiction by Paula Martin:
Bone by Bone: A Love Story (2017)

This collection was born in the cold days and long nights between the Winter Solstice and the Spring Equinox as the earth was healing, dreaming, and mirroring the importance of going inward, whispering ancient secrets and long-forgotten truths, and, like a wise elder, telling stories to those who would listen.

.

I.

Last night stones sang me
to sleep, their soft, haunting lullabies
surrounded by the dust of
my ancestors' bones, melodies
older than the redwood's lofty
poem, the mountain's
star-kissed cheek.

I tried to stay awake, hold
their words like a baby bird
in my cupped palm,
but their ancient harmonies lulled
me and slipped soundlessly
through my fingers like
smooth, wet river rocks.

Tonight I wait for stones to again
sing me to sleep, aching
for their secrets to awaken
my remembering.

Maybe then I can finally
find my way home.

II.

I stand alone and ankle-deep in
the ancient river, my reflection
rippling like an echo, my breath
the cold, still space between stars.

In the distance I hear the honking
of geese as they take turns
leading each other home.

A silver sliver of moon lingers
in the December morning sky
like a lynx, silently watching,
keeper of secrets.

Heron footprints lead up the riverbank
so I turn and follow them, my soles
shifting in soft sand.

I reach down and pick up a feather,
slate blue of the winter sky, and sense
him gliding behind me to the river's
edge, stepping where I had stood.

I turn just in time to see his beak pierce
the surface, then the silvery glint
of a wriggling fish.

III.

I watch through the kitchen window
like a voyeur as a flush of pink spreads
upward from the horizon,
the sky blushing as the sun rises
like a savior and streaks of pink
deepen to purple like passion
marks on a lover's neck.

The air is cold, sacred, the last breath
before a first kiss.

I feel giddy, enchanted, teetering
on the cusp of Holiness.
Creation.
Truth.

I catch sight of my reflection
in the frosted glass, looking outside
for what I have forgotten
I have within.

IV.

Doubt swirls in my mind
like a cold, restless wind,
rustling bare branches,
stirring up dirt.

My eyes are drawn to the clouds,
white, heavy with child
as they flow gently east
in a slow-moving sea.

Then snow fills the sky
with soft, silent poems,
rendering words useless,
inspiring the world mute.

V.

I sit on the riverbank
as the sun slips behind
the pines like a shy lover,

the sky the iridescent pink
of a mussel's secret, the moon
a smooth, white pearl.

Stories breathe in the air
around me, warm,
damp against my cheek.

A whisper flitters by me
like a moth, so I close
my eyes, hold my breath like a child.

My bones begin to vibrate outward
like sonar, but the echo is empty.
Bloodless. Silent.

I finally exhale, open my eyes.
My rippling reflection watches
me from the water's surface,

the sky the iridescent pink
of a mussel's secret, the moon
a smooth, white pearl.

VI.

I hear the creek singing like a distant
star, melodies flowing under thin ice,
ancient songs unseen.

I'm surrounded by bare branches, death
crunches underfoot. The goddess sleeps
soundly under a blanket of frost.

My eyes catch a glimmer warmed by
the sun, dissolving the barrier, rising
to the surface.

I sit on cold soil, close my eyes,
listen. My breath crystalizes
in glistening galaxies between us.

VII.

The sun rises behind
a blanket of grey,
the sky damp, drained of color.

We are stripped, bare,
stuck waiting between
winter and spring.

Suddenly there's movement
so I turn with heavy
head, slow eyes.

A cardinal, impossibly red,
jumps and then soars,
wings lifted

by invisible air, crest
pointing to concealed stars
like a prophet.

VIII.

The afternoon breeze, unseasonably
warm, caresses my skin
with teases, enchants.

I feel my pulse quicken, my shoulders
relax. The sun kisses my ear,
whispers, "Winter has passed."

Earth catches my eye, sleeping, biding
her time. Leaves hollowed brown.
Emptied. Free of regret.

I slow down and listen to the breathing
of trees. The cold wind waits patiently
shaded in shadows.

IX.

I walk alone, tired,
the world quiet. Too bright.
The earth sleeps, frozen,
a harsh layer of cold.

Cracks spread in my mind
like webs on thin ice.
Shoulders curve against wind,
bare feet on white snow.

Then suddenly a murmur
from deep within warmth,
wordless words rising up
through my soles like thin smoke.

I stop, my cells humming,
and melt into Her,
awake and singing
like the space between stars.

X.

I wake from a midmorning dream
of water collecting in pools,
my body storing joules like
a pocketful of stones.

Fog has floated in on a whisper,
shadowed hard angles.
The bare oak sleeps, dormant,
the sun a faraway star.

Green sprouts from dead leaves,
overly eager for growth,
risking life for light
before tonight's certain freeze.

I turn away from the window,
cocoon back in my covers,
close my eyes, float weightlessly
into an inky-black sleep.

XI.

The moon is full,
glowing, the milky
eye of a crone.
Her gaze is ancient, watching,
knower of secrets,
illuminator of shadows.
Stars pale as she rises
and mirrors back
my own light, beckoning me
to recognize my reflection.
I take a deep breath
and let go, allow her light
to guide me−

gentle, salty, a wave
kissing the shore.

XII.

Dawn is quiet, sleepy, suspended in
time. Space.

I sit on the edge of the river, the water
caressing my feet, lingering like a secret.

Fog surrounds me in a whisper, softens
my vision, a thin veil between worlds.

I sense her before I see her, the curve
of her neck, her milky white plumes.

She rises from the mist like a goddess,
wings opening to a hidden sun, feathers

damp with promise.

XIII.

For the third morning in a row
she watches from the shadows
as her dream shimmers in the east
eave of my porch, dew glistening
on silk threads like strands
of translucent pearls.

Her nightly weaving complete,
she is resting. Waiting. Being.

In the light of today's sun
she will allow the intricate patterns
that she birthed in darkness to attract
abundance, provide her sustenance.

Then, when the light is low
and she is replenished, she will ingest
today's threads, transmuting them
to tomorrow's dream.

And when my eave is clean
and clear, tonight, under
the darkness of the new moon,
she will begin again.

XIV.

Last night I dreamed the sky
was filled with starlings,
murmuration flowing like water,
shapeshifting as one.

A hawk's call pierced the barrier
as she hunted for prey. I woke
trembling, alone, my breath caught
in my throat.

I turned toward my window,
watched her soar overhead,
her graceful wings floating, circles
pulling me upward.

XV.

I watch through the window as
the redbud stands naked
in my front yard, her branches
stripped bare by frigid winds,
the last of her leaves reduced
to soft, brown dirt.

I fear she didn't survive the winter.

If I could become a child again
I could hear her singing, recognize
her secret. But it was a long, cold
winter, and I am tired.

If I only knew now that, despite
my lack of faith,
next week she'll fulfill
her promise in ecstatic pink bursts,
and I will stumble out of the darkness,
shake out my tangled hair, rise with her
as she awakens.

And when the time comes
for her petals to soften, release,
and take flight,
so will I.

XVI.

My yard is fat, wet,
swollen with storms.

Yesterday flows downhill,
collects in pools.

Clouds rumble and flash,
threaten the sun.

Seeds grow quietly under mud,
gathering strength to rise.

XVII.

The trail is slick, muddy,
still cold from the melted snow
as my feet stick, pull, leave behind
temporary prints.

Sunlight dances on the damp
forest floor as a circle
of towering pines
sways in the breeze,
whispering and giggling
like elderly sisters.

In my mind's eye
I see the dust of my ancestors
flowing from roots through
concentric rings, rising
to the highest branch,
floating on wings of first flight.

I walk to the center of the circle
then around, clockwise,
my fingerprints brushing
ancient bark, my shed cells
absorbing then spiraling
higher and higher
toward the sun.

XVIII.

3am and the moon shines
through my window like a searchlight,
forcing me awake.

In the distance the owl's call
rises and soars over treetops,
ready to lead me home.

I'm not ready I whisper
as the moon insists
that I waken. Reflect. Shine.

I take a deep breath, sit up
in bed like a child. Then I accept
the light, unfurl my wings,

and fly.

About the Author

Paula Martin was born in Pine Bluff, Arkansas and spent her formative years in Little Rock. She received her MFA in creative writing from the University of New Orleans before going on to create and produce the internationally-syndicated *Tales from the South* radio show. A recipient of the Arkansas Arts Council Governor's Arts Award, and the 2017 Inductee into the Arkansas Writers' Hall of Fame, Paula is the author of the novels *broken water* and *Bone by Bone: A Love Story* and lives in Little Rock with her three children.

Other titles by
EARTH SONGS PRESS
www.earthsongspress.com

Plant Spirit Totems by Bloom Post

Bone by Bone: A Love Story by Paula Martin

End to Ending: an AT Thru-Hiker's Story by Tanner Critz

Healing Presence by Joanna J. Seibert

Locally Grown by Annamary Thompson

Remembering the Truth by Janice Krasselt Tatter

Snapshots of Vietnam by James F. March

The Call of the Psalms by Joanna J. Seibert

A Rain Falling Star by Thea Kay Leopoulos

Bridges: Anthology of Short Stories edited by Maurice Lee

Taste and See by Joanna J. Seibert and Joanna E. Seibert

broken water by Paula Martin Morell

www.ingramcontent.com/pod-product-compliance
Lightning Source LLC
Chambersburg PA
CBHW050949030426
42339CB00007B/350